Congressional
Research Service
Informing the legislative debate since 1914

Housing Issues in the 113th Congress

Katie Jones, Coordinator
Analyst in Housing Policy

David H. Carpenter
Legislative Attorney

Sean M. Hoskins
Analyst in Financial Economics

Mark P. Keightley
Specialist in Economics

Maggie McCarty
Specialist in Housing Policy

N. Eric Weiss
Specialist in Financial Economics

July 8, 2014

Congressional Research Service

7-5700

www.crs.gov

R43367

Summary

The 113th Congress has been active in considering a number of housing-related issues. In general, the issues that have been of interest to Congress can be divided into two broad categories: (1) issues related to homeownership and financing home purchases, and (2) issues related to housing assistance programs for low-income households. Housing assistance for low-income households tends to be primarily, but not exclusively, related to rental housing.

During the 113th Congress, housing and mortgage markets have been showing some signs of recovering after several years of distress. Nevertheless, several issues that Congress has been considering are related to addressing problems that arose from the turmoil in housing and mortgage markets in recent years. Congress has also been considering policy changes designed to address problems that are perceived to have contributed to the housing downturn in an attempt to avoid a similar situation in the future.

One major issue that has been on Congress's agenda is reform of the housing finance system. Specifically, Congress has been considering measures to wind down and possibly replace Fannie Mae and Freddie Mac, two government-sponsored enterprises (GSEs) that purchase mortgages and package them into guaranteed mortgage-backed securities. Congress has also been considering reforms to the Federal Housing Administration (FHA), both as part of larger housing finance reform proposals and as stand-alone measures, in light of concerns about FHA's finances. Additionally, Congress has been interested in overseeing the implementation of several mortgage-related rulemakings that were enacted as part of the Dodd-Frank Wall Street Reform and Consumer Protection Act (P.L. 111-203) in the 111th Congress, as well as deliberating on other issues related to housing finance.

Congress has also been considering a number of issues related to housing assistance for low-income individuals and families. In recent years, housing affordability issues have become more prevalent, partly due to the effects of the economic recession. At the same time, in response to growing concerns about the long-term budget outlook, less funding has been provided for many of the housing assistance programs administered by the Department of Housing and Urban Development (HUD). Therefore, an issue before Congress has been how to prioritize funding for housing programs. Congress has also been considering additional issues related to housing for low-income families, including reforms to certain rental assistance programs and the reauthorization of the major federal program that provides federal housing assistance to low-income Native Americans living in tribal areas.

Congress has also been weighing whether to extend certain housing-related tax provisions that expired at the end of 2013, such as the tax exclusion for canceled mortgage debt income. The 113th Congress could also see the consideration of several additional housing-related tax provisions, including the mortgage interest deduction for homeowners or the low-income housing tax credit (LIHTC) for housing developers, as part of wider tax reform efforts.

Contents

Figures

Contacts

Introduction

Housing and mortgage markets in the United States have experienced significant turmoil in recent years. After several years of increasing, house prices began to decrease around 2006, contributing to increasing mortgage delinquency and foreclosure rates that reached historic levels. This turmoil had far-reaching implications for individual households and communities, as well as for the financial system and economy as a whole.

During the 113th Congress, housing markets have been showing signs of stabilizing, although concerns remain. Even though housing markets have shown some signs of improvement, Congress has continued to grapple with multiple issues related to the aftermath of this turmoil in housing and mortgage markets. These issues have included considering large-scale reforms to the housing finance system and overseeing the implementation of new rules related to mortgage lending that were enacted in response to issues that were perceived to have contributed to the housing market collapse.

Even as the economy recovers, lower-income households, who are more likely to be renters, may find it more difficult to find adequate, affordable housing. Furthermore, in response to concerns about the long-term budget outlook, Congress has been providing less funding for many domestic discretionary programs, including housing programs primarily administered by the Department of Housing and Urban Development (HUD). In this light, Congress has been considering issues such as how to prioritize funding for housing assistance programs in an environment of fiscal austerity, as well as possible reforms to certain housing assistance programs.

This report begins by providing an overview of the current state of housing markets (both homeownership and rental) and the mortgage market in order to provide context for the policy issues that have been active during the 113th Congress. It then provides a brief description of issues that the 113th Congress has been considering. These issues are broadly divided into two categories: issues related to homeownership and housing finance, and issues related to housing assistance for low-income households. This report is meant to provide a broad overview of the issues and is not intended to provide detailed information or analysis. However, this report does include references to other, more in-depth CRS reports on the issues when possible.

Background on Housing Conditions

Housing Markets

Housing markets are local, rather than national, in nature, and therefore housing markets might vary dramatically across the country. Nonetheless, on a national level, many housing indicators have been showing positive signs during the 113th Congress. In homeownership markets, home sales and home prices increased in 2013. This, in turn, can have a number of positive economic effects, including reducing the number of homeowners who owe more on their mortgages than their homes are worth and leading to an increase in construction activity. However, rising home prices and increasing interest rates, combined with relatively tight credit standards, may make it more difficult for some prospective homebuyers to buy homes.

Rental markets have generally been tightening, meaning that rents have been rising and vacancy rates falling. This may make it more difficult for some families, particularly those at the lower end of the income scale, to find adequate, affordable rental housing.

Homeownership Markets

On a national basis, homeownership markets have shown signs of strengthening after several years of weakness. In 2013, house prices increased, foreclosure rates decreased, and home sales increased slightly from their levels in recent years. However, during the first several months of 2014, some housing indicators were lower than they had been during the same period of 2013, raising concerns that the housing recovery could slow.[1] For example, new and existing home sales and housing starts were lower in early 2014 than they had been during the same period in 2013.[2] It remains to be seen whether home sales and housing starts will remain on pace to end the year below their 2013 levels or if their performance will improve over the course of the year.

Home Prices

Nationally, home prices began to rise again in the beginning of 2012 after several years of declines. **Figure 1** shows the rate of change in house prices in each quarter from the same quarter a year earlier. As the figure shows, between 2000 and 2007, house prices consistently increased compared to the same period in the previous year, although towards the end of that time period house prices increased at lower rates than they had during the beginning of the period. Beginning in late 2007, house prices began to decline on a year over year basis, and continued to do so for several years before beginning to increase once again in early 2012.

Home prices began to rise on a national level again in 2012, and in each quarter in 2013 house prices increased by between 7% and 8.5% over the same quarters in 2012. This rate of increase in house prices is the largest increase seen since mid-2006. However, in many markets, home prices are still well below what they were at their peak. Furthermore, while house prices continued to increase into the first quarter of 2014, the rate of year-over-year house price appreciation was slightly lower in the fourth quarter of 2013 and the first quarter of 2014 than it had been in previous quarters.

While rising house prices are good for existing homeowners, and can have positive effects on the economy as a whole, they can also have the effect of making homeownership less affordable for prospective homebuyers.

---

[1] For example, see the May 7, 2014, testimony of Federal Reserve Chair Janet Yellen before the Joint Economic Committee, stating that a possible risk to the economy "is that the recent flattening out in housing activity could prove more protracted than currently expected rather than resuming its earlier pace of recovery," at http://www.federalreserve.gov/newsevents/testimony/yellen20140507a htm.

[2] Freddie Mac June 2014 U.S. Economic & Housing Market Outlook, "2014: A Mid-Year Assessment," http://www.freddiemac.com/finance/pdf/June_2014_public_outlook.pdf.

Figure 1. Year-Over-Year House Prices Changes

(Q1 2000–Q1 2014)

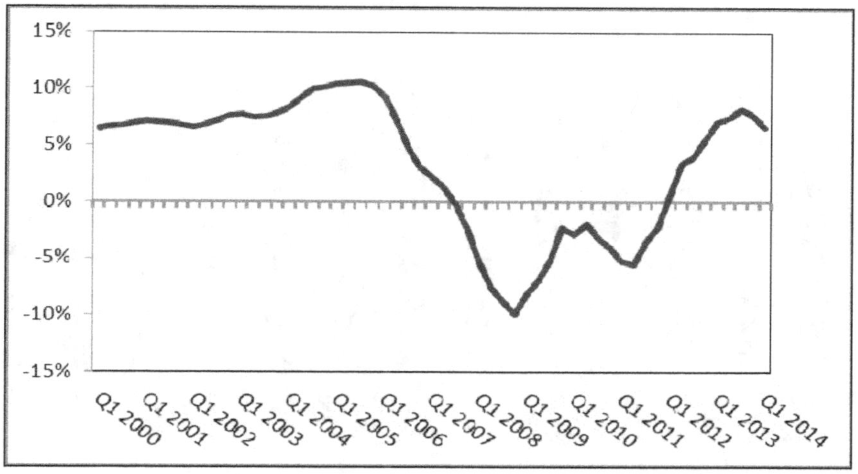

Source: Figure created by CRS using data from the Federal Housing Finance Agency House Price Index, (Seasonally Adjusted Purchase-Only Index).

Housing Equity

Rising home prices are having the effect of reducing the number of people who owe more on their mortgages than their homes are worth, referred to as being in a negative equity position. Negative equity can impact homeowners' ability to avoid foreclosure if they experience income shocks or limit a household's ability to move in response to a change in circumstances.

CoreLogic, a real estate data firm, reported that rising home prices helped 4 million homeowners reach positive equity in 2013.[3] As **Figure 2** shows, the percentage of mortgaged homes with negative equity has decreased to less than 13% in the first quarter of 2014, down from highs of about 25% as recently as the fourth quarter of 2011. Still, about 6.3 million homeowners remain in negative equity positions.[4]

---

[3] *CoreLogic Equity Report, Fourth Quarter 2013*, p. 2, http://www.corelogic.com/research/negative-equity/corelogic-q4-2013-equity-report.pdf. According to the report, 6.4 million properties had negative equity in the fourth quarter of 2013, compared to 10.5 million properties in the fourth quarter of 2012.

[4] *CoreLogic Equity Report, First Quarter 2014*, p. 8, http://www.corelogic.com/research/negative-equity/corelogic-q1-2014-equity-report.pdf.

Figure 2. Percentage of Mortgaged Homes with Negative Equity
(QI 2011-QI 2014)

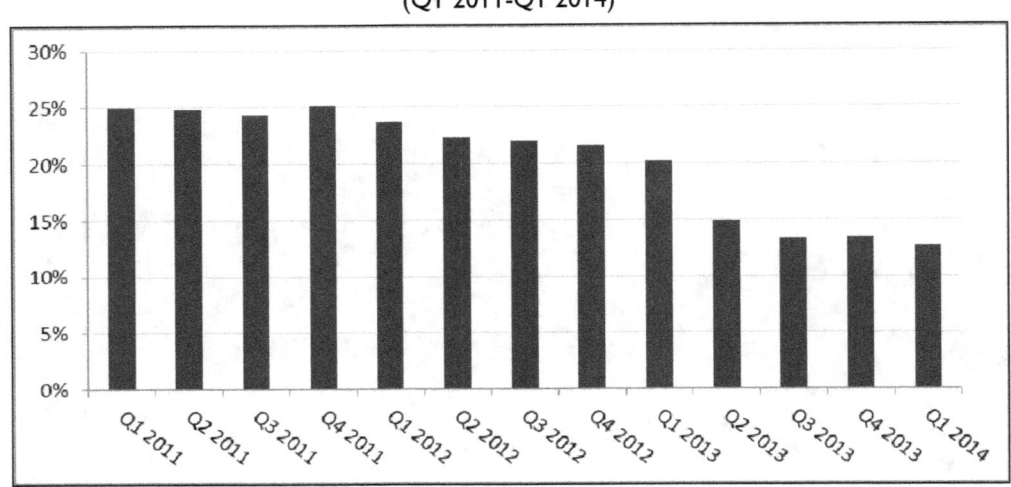

Source: Figure created by CRS using data from *CoreLogic Equity Report, First Quarter 2014*, http://www.corelogic.com/research/negative-equity/corelogic-q1-2014-equity-report.pdf.

While the overall percentage of mortgaged homes in negative equity positions has been decreasing, the share of mortgaged homes with negative equity varies widely by state. In the first quarter of 2014, Nevada had the highest share of mortgaged homes with negative equity (29%), while Texas had the smallest share (3%).[5]

Home Sales

As home prices rise, more homeowners may decide to put their homes on the market, increasing the supply of homes for sale. As shown in **Figure 3** and **Figure 4**, sales of both existing homes and new homes remain well below the levels they were at prior to the housing market turmoil of recent years, but they have begun to increase slightly on a year-to-year basis. The number of existing home sales in 2013 was nearly 5.1 million, up from 4.6 million in 2012 and 4.3 million in 2011. The number of new home sales in 2013 was over 400,000, up from 370,000 in 2012.[6]

Although home sales have been rising modestly in the last few years, home sales during the first several months of 2014 were lower than anticipated. Some analysts have predicted that the overall number of home sales in 2014 may not exceed the number of home sales in 2013.[7]

---

[5] *CoreLogic Equity Report, First Quarter 2014*, page 10.

[6] Due to differences in definitions and the timing of reporting, existing home sales and new home sales are not directly comparable to one another. For more information, see http://www.census.gov/construction/nrs/new_vs_existing.html.

[7] For example, see the Freddie Mac U.S. Economic and Housing Market Outlook for June 2014: "Home sales are likely to be a bit below the 5.5 million pace from last year ... we're lowering our overall home sales forecast from 5.5 million to 5.4 million."

Figure 3. Existing Home Sales
(in thousands)

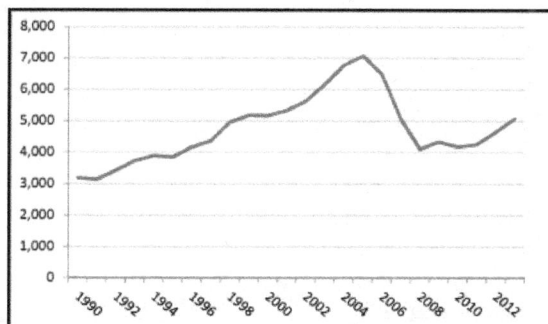

Source: Figure created by CRS using data from the National Association of Realtors, as reported in HUD's U.S. Housing Market Conditions Report for the fourth quarter of 2013.

Figure 4. New Home Sales
(in thousands)

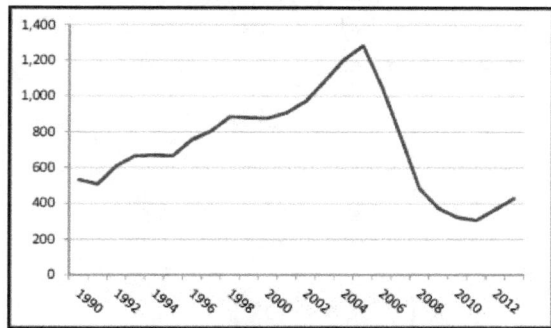

Source: Figure created by CRS using data from U.S. Census Bureau, New Residential Sales Historical Data.

Housing Starts

The number of home sales is important because, among other things, it can affect new housing construction. When the demand for homes exceeds the supply of available homes on the market—either due to increasing demand from homebuyers or a low inventory of homes for sale—then new homes may be built to meet the demand. Construction of new homes can be an important contributor to the economy and create jobs.

According to Census data, and as shown in **Figure 5**, housing starts in one-unit residential buildings were generally between about 1.2 million and 1.6 million per year between 2000 and 2007, reaching a peak of 1.7 million in 2005. Since that time, however, housing starts fell to 600,000 per year in 2008 and under 500,000 per year in each of the next three years. In 2012, housing starts in one-unit buildings showed a slight uptick, increasing to over 500,000, and in 2013 housing starts exceeded 600,000. However, they remain well below the levels seen throughout the 1990s and 2000s.

Figure 5. New Housing Starts Per Year, 1990-2013

(in thousands of units)

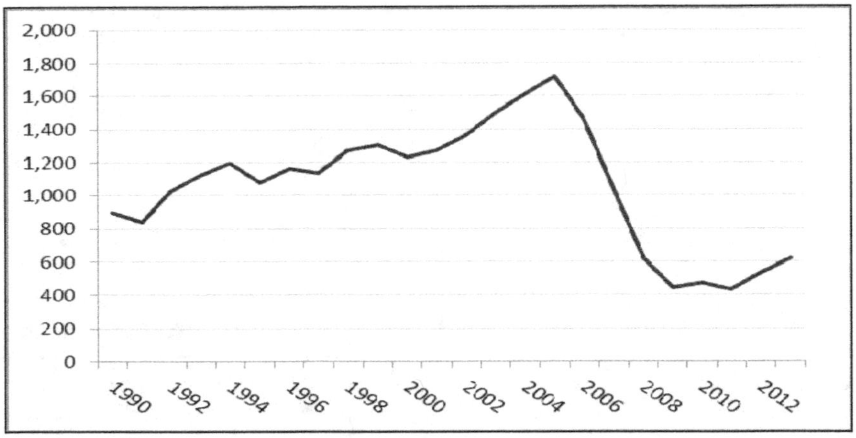

Source: Figure created by CRS using Census Bureau data on New Privately Owned Housing Units Started, Annual Data, available at http://www.census.gov/construction/nrc/historical_data/.

Notes: Data are for one-unit buildings only.

Mortgage Delinquency and Foreclosure Rates

Delinquency and foreclosure rates began to increase dramatically in the United States beginning in the middle of 2006, and have remained at elevated levels since then. However, over the last year, they have shown signs of beginning to decrease as fewer mortgages have become delinquent and entered the foreclosure process. Foreclosure completions on some mortgages that have been in the foreclosure process for an extended period of time may also be contributing to the decrease in the share of mortgages that are in the foreclosure process.

Figure 6 shows the percentage of all mortgages that were in the foreclosure inventory—meaning that they were in some stage of the foreclosure process—in each quarter since the beginning of 2001. The foreclosure inventory rate is currently under 3%, down from a peak of nearly 5%.

Figure 6. Foreclosure Inventory Rates

(QI 2001–QI 2014)

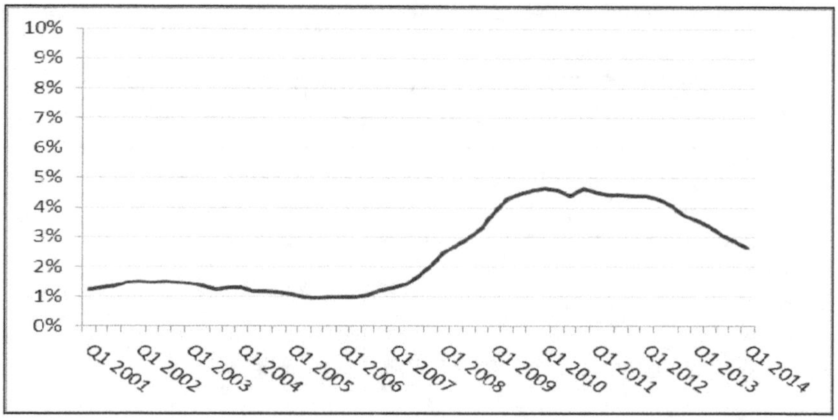

Source: Figure created by CRS using data from the Mortgage Bankers Association's National Delinquency Survey.

Notes: Foreclosure inventory rates are the percentage of mortgages that were in some stage of the foreclosure process as of the last day of the quarter.

Rental Markets

In 2013, there were about 40 million units of renter-occupied housing nationwide, and renters accounted for about 35% of all occupied housing units.[8] Over one-third of rental housing is in one-unit structures, and nearly 60% is in single-family (1-4 unit) structures. Thirty percent of rental housing is in buildings with 10 or more units.[9] In general, renter households are younger, smaller, more likely to be minorities, and have lower incomes than owner households.[10]

The number of households that rent their homes has been increasing in recent years.[11] During the 113th Congress, rental markets across the country have generally been tightening, meaning that rents are rising and vacancy rates are falling.[12]

Rental and Vacancy Rates

The share of renters relative to owners has been increasing in recent years. As shown in **Figure 7**, from 2004 to 2006, rates of renters fell to a historic low of 31% as homeownership rates reached historic highs.[13] Today, homeownership rates have fallen and rates of rental occupancy are up to

---

[8] U.S. Census Bureau, *Annual Housing Vacancy and Homeownership Survey*, Table 11. Estimates of the Total Housing Inventory of the United States: 2012 and 2013.

[9] U.S. Census Bureau, *Annual Housing Vacancy and Homeownership Survey*, Table 2. Rental and Homeownership Vacancy Rates, by Selected Characteristics and Percent Distribution of All Units: 2012 and 2013.

[10] Beekman Advisors, "Primer on Multifamily Housing & Finance," July 31, 2013, adapted from 2011 American Housing Survey National Summary Report and 2011 American Community Survey 1 Year Estimates.

[11] Joint Center for Housing Studies, The State of the Nation's Housing, 2013, http://www.jchs harvard.edu/sites/ jchs harvard.edu/files/son2013_chap5_rental_housing.pdf.

[12] Ibid.

[13] U.S. Department of Housing and Urban Development, *U. S. Housing Market Conditions Report, National Housing Market Summary and Data*. Data are adapted from, U.S. Census Bureau, *Annual Housing Vacancy and* (continued...)

about 35%, a rate not seen since 1996 and about equal to the historic average (35% from 1965-present).[14] This increase is at least partly attributable to the lingering effects of the economic downturn of 2007-2009.[15]

Figure 7. Rental and Homeownership Rates

(1965-2013)

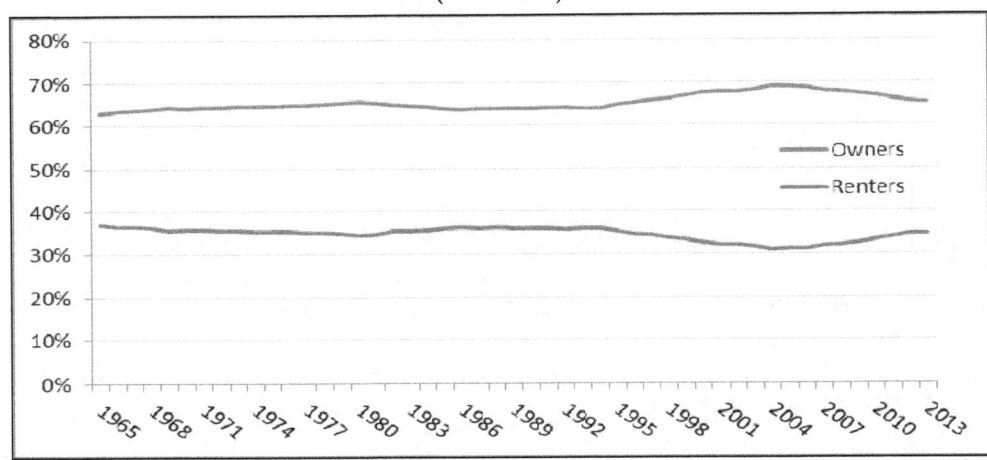

Source: Chart prepared by CRS based on data from U.S. Department of Housing and Urban Development, *U. S. Housing Market Conditions Report, National Housing Market Summary and Data.* Data are adapted from, U.S. Census Bureau, *Annual Housing Vacancy and Homeownership Survey,* Table 14. Homeownership Rates for the US and Regions: 1965 to Present.

Although some previously owner-occupied single-family housing has been converted to rental housing in recent years, the increasing number of renter households has led to lower vacancy rates, indicating a tightening of the rental market. As **Figure 8** shows, rental vacancy rates, after a period of historic highs, have now fallen to pre-recession levels.

(...continued)

Homeownership Survey, Table 14. Homeownership Rates for the US and Regions: 1965 to Present.

[14] Ibid.

[15] Harvard Joint Center for Housing Studies, *State of the Nation's Housing 2012 Report*, Chapter 4: Homeownership.

Figure 8. Rental Vacancy Rates

(1979-2013)

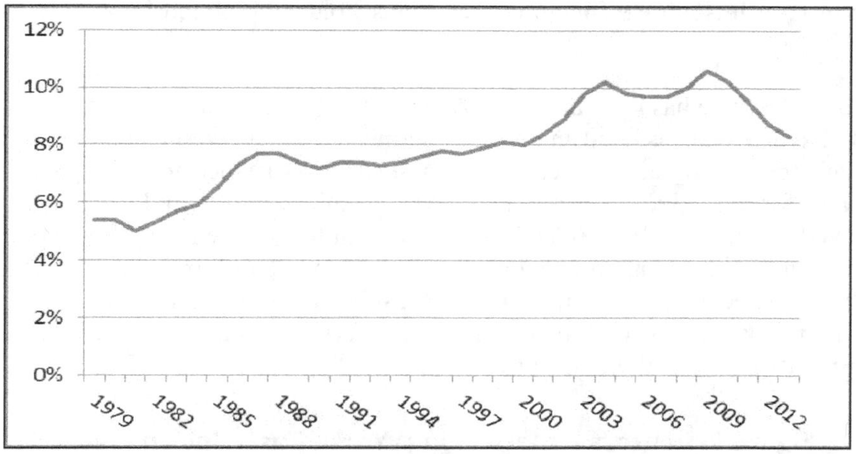

Source: Chart prepared by CRS using data from U.S. Department of Housing and Urban Development, *U. S. Housing Market Conditions Report, National Housing Market Summary and Data.* Data are adapted from, U.S. Census Bureau, *Annual Housing Vacancy and Homeownership Survey,* Table 1. Quarterly Rental Vacancy Rates: 1956 to Present.

Rents

With vacancy rates falling, rents have been increasing. According to data from the U.S. Census Bureau, the median asking rent for a vacant rental unit in 2013 was $734 per month.[16] Nominal rents increased by 2.8% in 2013, similar to their rate of increase in 2012.[17] Rents are increasing in most areas of the country; according to Harvard's Joint Center for Housing Studies *State of the Nation's Housing Report,* research by MPF Research showed rents increasing during 2013 in 85 of 93 metropolitan areas that were included in its research, although the rate of increases slowed in many areas.[18]

Affordability

In the aftermath of the 2007-2009 recession, many households have experienced joblessness or income loss. Renters' incomes have generally not kept pace with increases in rents, and rental housing affordability may be an issue for many households. One common definition of affordability classifies housing as affordable if a household is paying no more than 30% of its income in housing costs. Under this definition, households that pay more than 30% of income for housing are considered to be cost-burdened, and households that pay more than 50% of their income for housing costs are considered to be severely cost-burdened.

According to the Joint Center for Housing Studies, citing data from the American Community Survey, about half of all renters—a total of 21 million households—were cost-burdened in

---

[16] U.S. Census Bureau, *Annual Housing Vacancy and Homeownership Survey,* Table 12. Vacant For-Rent Units, by Selected Characteristic for the United States: 1960, 1970, 1975, and 1980 to 2013.

[17] Harvard Joint Center for Housing Studies, *State of the Nation's Housing 2014 Report,* Chapter 5: Rental Housing, page 23.

[18] Ibid.

2012.[19] The share of renters paying more than 30% of their income for housing costs is increasing at all income levels.[20] Not surprisingly, however, lower-income households are the most likely to be cost-burdened, as it is more difficult for these households to find housing that costs less than 30% of their incomes.

According to HUD, there has been an over 20% increase in the number of renters who are considered to have "worst case housing needs," defined as renters with incomes at or below 50% of area median income who do not receive federal housing assistance and who pay more than half of their incomes for rent, live in severely inadequate conditions, or both. In 2011, the most recent year for which data are available, HUD found that 8.5 million households were experiencing worst-case housing needs, compared to 7 million in 2009 and 6 million in 2007.[21] This increase in worst-case housing needs is shown in **Figure 9**. Most households experiencing worst case housing needs are cost burdened; only 3% of households experiencing worst case housing needs live in housing that is physically inadequate.[22]

Figure 9. Renters Experiencing Worst-Case Housing Needs

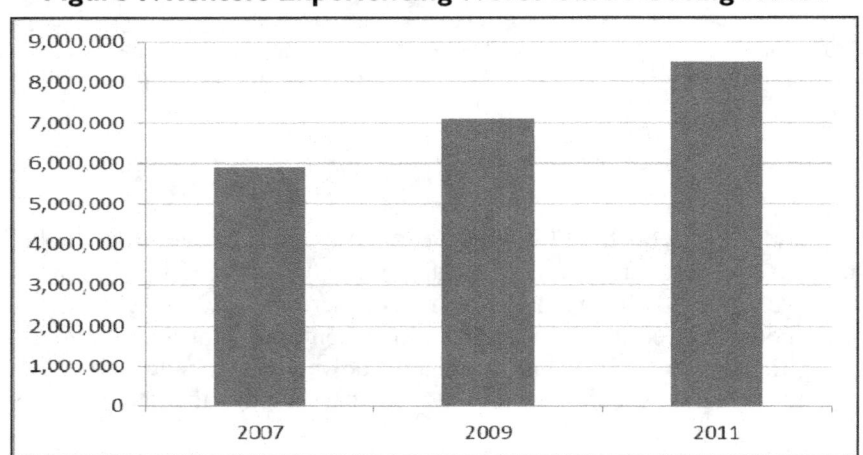

Source: U.S. Department of Housing and Urban Development, *Worst Case Housing Needs 2011: Report to Congress*, August 2013, p. vii.

Notes: HUD defines worst-case housing needs as renter households with incomes at or below 50% of the area median income who are not receiving federal housing assistance and pay more than half of their incomes for rent, live in housing that is severely physically inadequate, or both.

The Mortgage Market

Since the collapse of the housing "bubble," the mortgage market has been characterized by less mortgage credit availability. Many lenders and private mortgage insurers have tightened their

---

[19] Joint Center for Housing Studies, "America's Rental Housing," December 9, 2013, page 28, http://www.jchs harvard.edu/americas-rental-housing.

[20] Ibid., page 30.

[21] U.S. Department of Housing and Urban Development, Office of Policy Development and Research, "Worst Case Housing Needs 2011: Report to Congress," p. viii, http://www huduser.org/Publications/pdf/HUD-506_WorstCase2011_reportv3.pdf.

[22] Ibid., p. 2.

underwriting standards for mortgages, making it difficult for some prospective homebuyers to qualify or increasing the costs of a mortgage.[23] Some observers have expressed concerns that new mortgage rules could limit access to mortgages for some potential borrowers or that mortgage credit might be less available due in part to regulatory uncertainty. Several—but not all—new federal regulations related to mortgage lending that were mandated by the Dodd-Frank Wall Street Reform and Consumer Protection Act (Dodd-Frank Act, P.L. 111-203) were finalized in 2013 and went into effect in early 2014, potentially reducing uncertainty among lenders. On the demand side, economic factors have depressed household formation, reducing demand from first time homebuyers, and decreased home prices and the resultant negative equity have limited existing homebuyers' ability to "move up" in the market and buy larger homes.

Mortgage Market Composition

The mortgage market in recent years has largely consisted of mortgages insured by government agencies, such as the Federal Housing Administration (FHA), or purchased by Fannie Mae and Freddie Mac, two government-sponsored enterprises (GSEs) that are currently under government control. The share of new mortgages backed by one of these entities has reached as high as about 90% in recent years. According to the Urban Institute, using data from Inside Mortgage Finance, over 60% of new residential mortgages originated in 2013 were backed by Fannie Mae or Freddie Mac, with FHA or the Department of Veterans Affairs (VA) insuring an additional 20%. The remaining mortgages were mostly held on bank balance sheets, with a small percentage (less than 1%) being securitized through private companies rather than Fannie Mae, Freddie Mac, or Ginnie Mae (which guarantees mortgage-backed securities made up of government-insured mortgages, such as FHA-insured mortgages). This breakdown is shown in **Figure 10**.

Figure 10. Share of Mortgage Originations by Type in 2013

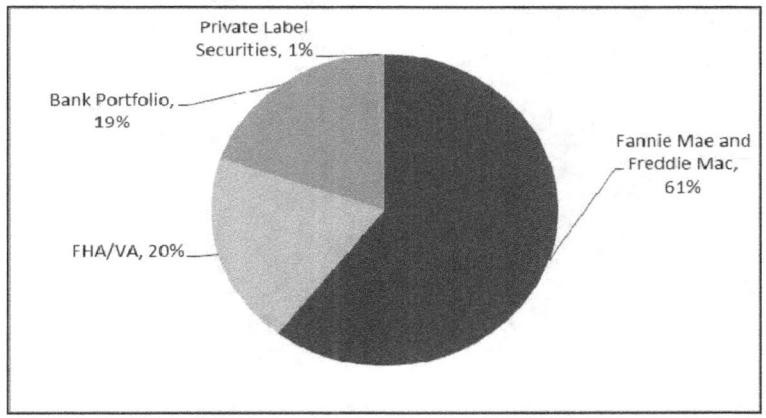

Source: Figure created by CRS using data from the Urban Institute Housing Finance Policy Center, *Housing Finance at a Glance: A Monthly Chartbook*, April 2014, p. 8, http://www.urban.org/UploadedPDF/413096-Housing-Finance-At-A-Glance-April-2014.pdf.

Notes: Figure shows share of first-lien mortgage originations.

---

[23] For example, see remarks given by Sandra Pianalto, President and CEO, Federal Reserve Bank of Cleveland, at the Ohio Housing Conference, November 6, 2013, stating "In a recent Federal Reserve survey of senior loan officers, bankers reported that credit standards for all categories of home mortgage loans have remained tighter than the standards that have prevailed on average since 2005." The full text of her remarks is available at http://www.clevelandfed.org/For_the_Public/News_and_Media/Speeches/2013/Pianalto_20131106b.cfm.

The high shares of mortgages being backed by the GSEs or by government mortgage insurance programs has led to debates about whether steps should be taken to reduce the government's role in the mortgage market, and, if so, what those steps should be and how quickly they should be taken. While some policy makers would like to see government agencies and the GSEs take steps to reduce their market share, such as raising fees or reducing the size of mortgages that they will guarantee, others policy makers have expressed concerns that such steps could reduce credit availability and make housing less affordable, possibly negatively impacting housing markets.

Interest Rates

Although mortgage lending has been tighter in recent years, interest rates have been historically low, possibly contributing to some households' decisions to obtain mortgages and contributing to higher rates of refinancing. As **Figure 11** illustrates, interest rates on 30-year fixed-rate mortgages have been under 5% since about May 2010, and were under 4% for most of 2012 and the first half of 2013.[24]

Interest rates started to slowly rise again in the second half of 2013 (although they remain under 5%), leading some to question whether rising interest rates might weaken the housing market by inhibiting home sales and refinancing activity. As rates begin to rise, fewer potential homebuyers might enter the market, and fewer households will be able to benefit from lowering their interest rate by refinancing. Rising interest rates could also deter some existing homeowners from selling their homes, since any new mortgages these homeowners obtained would likely have higher interest rates than what they are currently paying.

Although interest rates increased somewhat during 2013, as of May 2014 they had not increased above their December 2013 level. However, mortgage origination volumes were lower during the first several months of 2014 due to a decrease in refinancing activity.[25] Although interest rates remain low, many of the households that could benefit from refinancing into mortgages with lower interest rates may have already done so.

---

[24] These interest rates are from Freddie Mac's Primary Mortgage Market Survey, which reports average interest rates on a weekly basis based on a survey of lenders. The interest rates reported assume that the mortgage is a prime mortgage with an 80% loan-to-value ratio that meets Fannie Mae's and Freddie Mac's standards and is not government-insured. Actual interest rates charged to specific borrowers will depend on a variety of borrower and mortgage characteristics. For more information on the Primary Mortgage Market Survey, see Freddie Mac's website at http://www.freddiemac.com/pmms/abtpmms htm#8.

[25] For example, see the Urban Institute Housing Finance Policy Center, *Housing Finance at a Glance: A Monthly Chartbook, May 2014*, p. 12, http://www.urban.org/UploadedPDF/413127-Housing-Finance-At-A-Glance-May-2014.pdf.

Figure 11. Interest Rates on 30-Year Fixed-Rate Mortgages

(January 1999–May 2014)

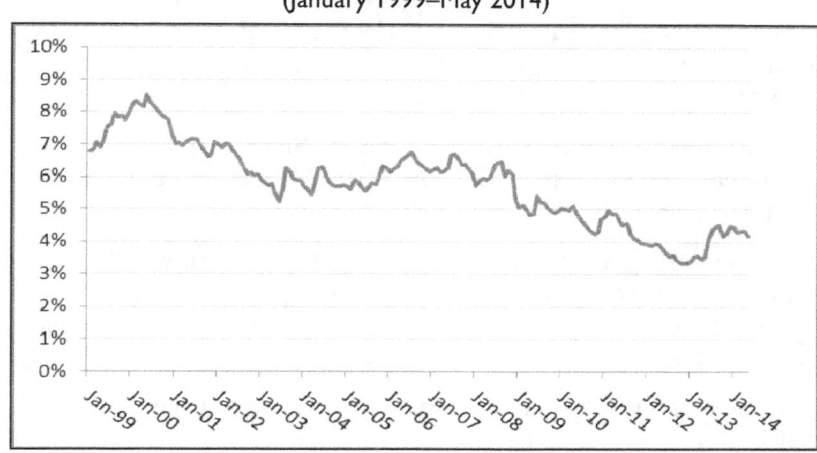

Source: Table created by CRS based on Freddie Mac Weekly Primary Mortgage Market Survey, 30-Year Fixed Rate Historic Tables, available at http://www.freddiemac.com/pmms/.

Issues Related to Housing Finance and Homeownership

A number of the housing issues that have been on the agenda of the 113th Congress have to do with housing finance or homeownership. One major issue that Congress has been considering is the possible large-scale reform of the housing finance system. Other housing finance-related issues on Congress's agenda have included deliberation on specific programs or policies that could have an impact on the availability or affordability of mortgages for certain households, including oversight of mortgage-related rulemakings and consideration of foreclosure prevention programs and policies.

Housing Finance Reform

As financial markets in general and the mortgage market in particular continue to recover from the 2007-2009 recession,[26] congressional interest has concentrated on reforming the housing finance system and determining the future role of the federal government in housing finance. Presently, the federal government guarantees and insures mortgages through the Federal Housing Administration (FHA), the Department of Veterans Affairs (VA), and the Department of Agriculture's rural housing programs. In addition, Fannie Mae and Freddie Mac, two congressionally chartered government-sponsored enterprises devoted to housing finance, are in conservatorship and have support contracts with the Department of the Treasury.

Discussions of housing finance reform have largely centered on the GSEs, although the role of FHA is also being debated. Among the goals of housing finance reform are:

---

[26] National Bureau of Economic Research, "US Business Cycle Expansions and Contractions" at http://www.nber.org/cycles html.

- Preventing taxpayers from having to provide assistance again in the future. To date, Treasury has invested $188 billion in Fannie Mae and Freddie Mac and received over $200 billion in dividends.[27] The Federal Reserve and Treasury provided additional support by purchasing bonds and mortgage-backed securities (MBS) issued by Fannie Mae and Freddie Mac.

- Returning private capital to the mortgage market. Since the recession, the government has directly or indirectly guaranteed 75% to 85% of mortgages originated.

- Ensuring that mortgages are available and affordable to creditworthy borrowers. In particular, there is concern that without government support for the mortgage market, homeowners will not have access to affordable, 30-year fixed rate, prepayable mortgages.

- Obtaining the best return on the funds already provided to Fannie Mae and Freddie Mac.

There have been several bills introduced to reform the housing finance system. Two bills that have been the subject of committee action are H.R. 2767, the Protecting American Taxpayers and Homeowners Act (the PATH Act),[28] in the House, and S. 1217, the Housing Finance Reform and Taxpayer Protection Act (commonly referred to as the Johnson-Crapo bill),[29] in the Senate.

In the House, the PATH Act proposes to wind down Fannie Mae and Freddie Mac over several years. It would replace them with a National Mortgage Market Utility that would facilitate mortgage securitization but would not provide a government guarantee. The act would also eliminate or delay the implementation of certain existing regulations that some believe are inhibiting the recovery in the mortgage market. In addition, as discussed in the following section, the PATH Act would reform the Federal Housing Administration (FHA), making it an independent agency and taking steps to improve its finances.

In the Senate, the Corker-Warner bill would wind down Fannie Mae and Freddie Mac and create the Federal Mortgage Insurance Corporation (FMIC) to oversee a new federal mortgage insurance program. The FMIC would be an independent agency charged with supporting the mortgage market and providing reinsurance on eligible mortgage-backed securities (MBS). These MBS would have an explicit full-faith-and-credit federal government guarantee, and the FMIC would regulate aspects of the mortgage market related to these MBS. Corker-Warner does not propose any changes to FHA, but another Senate bill (S. 1376), also discussed in the following section, would address FHA.

For more information on the current structure of the housing finance system, see CRS Report R42995, *An Overview of the Housing Finance System in the United States*, by Sean M. Hoskins,

---

[27] Dividend payments do not count toward paying back the amount injected by Treasury. Rather, the dividends compensate Treasury for its assistance and the risk it has assumed.

[28] H.R. 2767 was introduced on July 22, 2013, by Representative Scott Garrett. On July 24, 2013, it was ordered reported out of the House Financial Services Committee. It is also being considered by the House Committee on Ways and Means.

[29] S. 1217 was introduced on June 25, 2013, by Senator Bob Corker and referred to the Committee on Banking, Housing, and Urban Affairs. S. 1217, as introduced, is commonly referred to as the Corker-Warner bill. On May 15, 2014, S. 1217 was ordered to be reported with amendments by the Senate Committee on Banking, Housing, and Urban Affairs. S. 1217, as amended, is commonly referred to as the Johnson-Crapo bill.

Katie Jones, and N. Eric Weiss. For more information on the PATH Act and Corker-Warner, see CRS Report R43219, *Selected Legislative Proposals to Reform the Housing Finance System*, by Sean M. Hoskins, N. Eric Weiss, and Katie Jones. For more information on the GSEs and general options for GSE reform, see CRS Report R40800, *GSEs and the Government's Role in Housing Finance: Issues for the 113th Congress*, by N. Eric Weiss.

Federal Housing Administration

FHA, an agency within HUD, insures private mortgage lenders against losses on certain mortgages. If a borrower of an FHA-insured mortgage does not repay the loan as promised, then FHA will repay the lender the remaining amount that it is owed. The provision of FHA insurance is intended to encourage lenders to offer affordable mortgages to households who otherwise may find it difficult to qualify for mortgages at affordable rates, such as households with small down payments. FHA's home mortgage insurance program is intended to be self-supporting and to pay for the costs of defaulted mortgages through fees, or premiums, that it charges to borrowers, rather than through appropriations.

In recent years, increasing foreclosure rates and falling home prices have led to large increases in the costs that FHA expects to incur on the loans that it currently insures. FHA, like all federal credit programs subject to the Federal Credit Reform Act of 1990, has permanent and indefinite budget authority to draw funds from Treasury to cover any unexpected increases in the cost of guaranteed loans. At the end of FY2013, FHA used this authority to receive $1.7 billion from Treasury to ensure that it had sufficient funds to cover all of its expected future losses. This was the first time that FHA has ever needed funds from Treasury for its home mortgage insurance program.

A number of bills have been introduced in the 113th Congress that would make changes to FHA. These bills are generally targeted at improving FHA's financial position, but would do so in different ways. Many of these bills include certain changes that FHA has requested, such as additional authority for monitoring FHA-approved lenders, which it says will help it to better manage the FHA insurance fund. These bills also include additional measures aimed at stabilizing FHA's finances, such as increasing the amount of capital reserves that it is required to hold and requiring FHA to take certain actions if its capital reserves fall below certain thresholds.

Additional, more far-reaching reforms to FHA are also included in the PATH Act, which, as described in the previous section, would reform the housing finance system more broadly. Among other things, the PATH Act would make FHA an independent agency (it is currently part of HUD), would limit FHA insurance specifically to mortgages for low- and moderate-income households and first-time homebuyers, and would gradually reduce the share of a mortgage that FHA can insure. Other FHA reform bills, such as the FHA Solvency Act (S. 1376), include changes that are aimed at ensuring that FHA's programs are financially sound, but do not focus on limiting FHA's market role or shifting risk to the private sector to the degree that the PATH Act does. Another bill that includes changes aimed at improving FHA's financial soundness, but not on limiting its market role, is the FHA Emergency Fiscal Solvency Act of 2013 (H.R. 1145), which is similar to bills that passed the House in recent Congresses.

The 113th Congress has also enacted a bill aimed at strengthening FHA's reverse mortgage program. Some of FHA's anticipated losses are attributable to these reverse mortgages that FHA insures, known as Home Equity Conversion Mortgages (HECMs). The 113th Congress enacted the Reverse Mortgage Stabilization Act of 2013 (P.L. 113-29), which gives FHA greater flexibility to make changes to the HECM program through administrative guidance in order to more quickly implement changes that are intended to reduce the riskiness of these mortgages.

For more information on the features of FHA-insured mortgages, see CRS Report RS20530, *FHA-Insured Home Loans: An Overview* , by Katie Jones. For more information on FHA's financial status, see CRS Report R42875, *FHA Single-Family Mortgage Insurance: Financial Status of the Mutual Mortgage Insurance Fund (MMI Fund)*, by Katie Jones. For more information on FHA policy changes and proposed legislation related to FHA, see CRS Report R43531, *FHA Single-Family Mortgage Insurance: Recent Policy Changes and Proposed Legislation*, by Katie Jones.

Oversight of Mortgage-Related Rulemakings

Financial regulators are continuing to implement several mortgage-related rulemakings that were required by the Dodd-Frank Act of 2011. The Consumer Financial Protection Bureau (CFPB) has issued rules related to, among other things, the ability to repay and qualified mortgage (QM) standards, homeownership counseling, escrow requirements, mortgage servicing, loan originator compensation, and mortgage disclosure forms.[30] In addition, six federal agencies[31] issued a revised proposed rule for credit risk retention and qualified residential mortgages (QRM). Regulators have issued additional mortgage-market rules besides those mentioned above.

While each of the rules is different, there are several policy issues that are common across each of the rules individually as well as of the rules collectively. For example, some lenders are concerned about the compliance costs associated with satisfying the new rules.[32] There are also questions about how the rules will affect credit availability for creditworthy borrowers.[33] The 113th Congress may address these and other policy concerns in its oversight of the financial regulators. Congress is also considering legislative proposals to repeal or modify some of the mortgage-market rulemakings. For example, the PATH Act, in addition to winding down the GSEs and reforming FHA, would repeal the credit risk retention requirement,[34] modify the definition of a qualified mortgage,[35] and delay the effective date of certain mortgage reform regulations,[36] among other things.

---

[30] For a list of CFPB regulations, see http://www.consumerfinance.gov/regulations/.

[31] The six agencies are the Office of the Comptroller of the Currency, the Federal Reserve, the Federal Deposit Insurance Corporation, the Federal Housing Finance Agency, the Securities and Exchange Commission, and the Department of Housing and Urban Development.

[32] American Bankers Association, "ABA Backgrounder: Mortgage Reform into 2014," September 2013, at https://www.aba.com/Press/Documents/MortgageReform2014.pdf.

[33] Center for Responsible Lending, "Government-Mandated Down Payment Standards Would Harm the Economy, Deny Homeownership to Credit-Worthy Families," August 15, 2013, at http://www responsiblelending.org/mortgage-lending/policy-legislation/congress/Government-Mandated-Down-Payment-Standards html.

[34] H.R. 2767 §407.

[35] H.R. 2767 §403.

[36] H.R. 2767 §406.

Foreclosure Mitigation

In response to elevated mortgage default and foreclosure rates in recent years, the federal government has established a number of temporary programs and policies intended to help certain households avoid foreclosure. These have included programs to encourage lenders to modify mortgages in ways that lower borrowers' monthly payments (such as the Home Affordable Modification Program, or HAMP) and programs to make it easier to help certain borrowers in negative equity positions to refinance their mortgages and thus lower their interest rates (such as the Home Affordable Refinance Program, or HARP, which is limited to mortgages backed by Fannie Mae or Freddie Mac where borrowers are current on their payments). The expiration date for many of these programs has been administratively extended; HAMP and HARP are both currently scheduled to remain in existence through 2015.

Several bills have been introduced in the 113th Congress that would attempt to further assist households who are in danger of foreclosure or otherwise struggling with payments that are deemed to be unaffordable. Many of these bills focus on expanding the ability of certain households to refinance their mortgages, even if they have negative equity or are otherwise unable to refinance their mortgages through traditional channels. For example, several bills (including H.R. 736, H.R. 1712, and S. 249) would make changes to HARP with the intention of expanding the number of people who would be eligible for the program. These bills would continue to limit HARP eligibility to borrowers whose mortgages are backed by Fannie Mae or Freddie Mac.[37] Another bill, S. 1373, would attempt to expand HARP-like refinancing to mortgages that are not currently backed by Fannie Mae or Freddie Mac or insured by a government agency.

For more information on foreclosure prevention programs, see CRS Report R40210, *Preserving Homeownership: Foreclosure Prevention Initiatives*, by Katie Jones.

Protecting Tenants at Foreclosure Act

Another temporary measure that was enacted in response to high mortgage foreclosure rates is the Protecting Tenants at Foreclosure Act, which was enacted as part of the Helping Families Save Their Homes Act of 2009 (P.L. 111-22). The law provides certain protections for renters who are living in properties that go through foreclosure. These protections include requiring the new property owner to comply with certain notice requirements before a tenant can be evicted and, in some cases, allowing tenants to remain in the property for the term of an existing lease.

The provisions of the Protecting Tenants at Foreclosure Act are slated to expire after December 31, 2014.[38] Legislation (H.R. 3543 and S. 1761) has been introduced in the 113th Congress to make the provisions of the Protecting Tenants at Foreclosure Act permanent.

---

[37] Through HARP, Fannie Mae and Freddie Mac purchase negative equity mortgages refinanced by private lenders if the mortgages meet certain criteria. The program is limited to mortgages backed by Fannie Mae and Freddie Mac because those entities already own the risk on such mortgages; allowing mortgages that are not already backed by Fannie Mae and Freddie Mac to refinance through HARP would make Fannie Mae and Freddie Mac newly responsible for the risk on those mortgages.

[38] The original sunset date was December 31, 2012, but it was extended to December 31, 2014, by §1484 of the Dodd-Frank Wall Street Reform and Consumer Protection Act.

Mortgage-Related Enforcement Actions, Lawsuits, and Settlements

Legal wrangling stemming from the mortgage crisis has affected virtually every type of player involved in the mortgage market during the run-up to the housing market crash. The resulting federal and state investigations, enforcement actions, and legal settlements, as well as private litigation have led to the transfer of tens of billions of dollars among market participants and governmental regulators.

For example, in the fall of 2010, the sworn statements of employees from several large mortgage servicers and other evidence that surfaced in various foreclosure-related litigation raised concerns that the companies were systematically engaged in mortgage documentation and procedural improprieties, especially when handling mortgages in default. These concerns provoked a number of state and federal regulators to initiate multiple investigations, enforcement actions, lawsuits, and legal settlement negotiations. Although the alleged servicer misconduct is a common thread in these regulatory actions, the legal authorities at the disposal of the regulators differ considerably, which has resulted in varied remedies.

Beginning in the fourth quarter of 2010, the federal banking regulators began on-site examinations of the foreclosure processes and governance protocols of more than a dozen servicers.[39] As a result of its findings, the banking regulators entered into binding consent orders in April 2011 with these mortgage servicers and several of the third-party service providers that the servicers used in various ways during foreclosure processes.[40] The consent orders require servicers to redress homeowners potentially harmed in the past, as well as to improve behavior going forward.[41]

Additionally, on February 8, 2012, 49 state attorneys general,[42] the Conference of State Bank Supervisors, the U.S. Department of Housing and Urban Development (HUD), the U.S. Department of the Treasury (Treasury), and the U.S. Department of Justice (DOJ) announced a "National Mortgage Settlement" covering certain legal claims against the top five mortgage servicers.[43] The settlement provides mortgage servicers some certainty regarding their legal liability, while securing approximately $25 billion in monetary relief for individuals who lost homes through foreclosure in recent years and current homeowners who are struggling to maintain monthly payments.

---

[39] *Correcting Foreclosure Practices,* Office of the Comptroller of the Currency, available at http://www.occ.gov/topics/ consumer-protection/foreclosure-prevention/correcting-foreclosure-practices html. The examined servicers were: Aurora Bank FSB, Bank of America, N.A., Citibank, N.A., EverBank, GMAC Mortgage, Goldman Sachs, HSBC Bank USA, N.A., JPMorgan Chase Bank, N.A., MetLife Bank, N.A., Morgan Stanley, PNC Bank, N.A., Sovereign Bank, SunTrust Bank, U.S. Bank, N.A., and Wells Fargo Bank, N.A.

[40] The third-parties with which consent orders were entered include Mortgage Electronic Registration Systems, Inc. (MERS); DocX, LLC; and Lender Processing Services, Inc.

[41] See *Correcting Foreclosure Practices,* Office of the Comptroller of the Currency, available at http://www.occ.gov/ topics/consumer-protection/foreclosure-prevention/correcting-foreclosure-practices html and *What You Need to Know: Independent Foreclosure Review,* Board of Governors of the Federal Reserve System, available at http://www.federalreserve.gov/consumerinfo/independent-foreclosure-review htm.

[42] The Oklahoma Attorney General entered into a separate settlement agreement. *Oklahoma Mortgage Settlement Information,* Okla. Office of the Attorney Gen., available at https://www.oag.ok.gov/oagweb nsf/mortgageinfo html.

[43] The five mortgage servicers are Ally Financial, Inc. (formerly GMAC, Inc.), Bank of America, Corp., Citigroup, Inc., JP Morgan Chase & Co., and Wells Fargo & Co. See the consent judgments against each company, at Exhibits F (release of federal claims) and G (release of state claims), available at http://www nationalmortgagesettlement.com/.

Other litigation, enforcement actions, and legal settlements have involved mortgage-related activities outside of the context of mortgage servicing. For example, on October 19, 2013, the Justice Department, acting through the Obama Administration's Financial Fraud Enforcement Task Force's RMBS Working Group,[44] announced that federal and state regulators and JPMorgan Chase & Co. had reached a legal settlement stemming from the company's "packaging, marketing, sale and issuance of residential mortgage-backed securities (RMBS)." As part of the agreement, JPMorgan is required to pay approximately $13 billion, which will take various forms including civil penalties, restitution, and consumer relief.[45]

Furthermore, through negotiated settlements and private lawsuits, entities that purchased mortgages in the secondary market are seeking indemnification from sellers for the losses suffered from mortgages that allegedly failed to meet the underwriting standards that were promised pursuant to sales contracts. For instance, the Federal Housing Finance Agency (FHFA), acting as conservator of Fannie Mae and Freddie Mac, has sued at least 18 mortgage companies for violations of state and federal securities laws primarily stemming from Fannie Mae and Freddie Mac's purchases of mortgage-backed securities in the mid-2000s.[46] The FHFA has settled with at least 14 of these companies for a combined total of more than $15 billion.[47] Additionally, mortgage brokers have been charged with money laundering and other fraudulent activity in violation of federal law; mortgage originators have been charged with violating fair lending laws for discriminating against protected classes in marketing and originating mortgages; and federal regulators have levied mortgage-related fraud charges against bank directors and officers.[48]

The 113th Congress has expressed ongoing interest in the oversight of these mortgage-related legal settlements.[49] Certain Members of Congress have also called on regulators to provide additional information related to some of these settlement actions,[50] including information related to changes to the April 2011 consent orders that the OCC and the Federal Reserve entered into with over a dozen mortgage servicers.[51]

For more information on some of the foreclosure procedural issues that initially prompted investigation, see CRS Report R41491, *"Robo-Signing" and Other Alleged Documentation Problems in Judicial and Nonjudicial Foreclosure Processes*, by David H. Carpenter. For more

---

[44] Financial Fraud Enforcement Task Force's RMBS Working Group, available at http://www.stopfraud.gov/rmbs html.

[45] For more information on the JPMorgan settlement, see CRS Legal Sidebar WSLG726, JPMorgan Enters a $13 Billion Settlement with Regulators, by David H. Carpenter.

[46] *FHFA's Update on Private Label Securities Actions: 2013 and 2014 Settlements and Remaining Cases*, Federal Housing Finance Agency, last updated April 29, 2014, available at http://www fhfa.gov/Media/PublicAffairs/Pages/FHFAs-Update-on-Private-Label-Securities-Actions.aspx.

[47] Ibid.

[48] See *Accomplishments under the Leadership of Attorney General Eric Holder*, U.S. Department of Justice, available at http://www.justice.gov/accomplishments/.

[49] For example, the Senate Banking Committee's Subcommittee on Housing, Transportation, and Community Development held a hearing on *Helping Homeowners Harmed by Foreclosures: Ensuring Accountability and Transparency in Foreclosure Reviews*, on April 17, 2013.

[50] See, for example, S. 1898, the Truth in Settlements Act of 2014.

[51] See, for example, *House Oversight Committee Requests Briefing on Potential Independent Foreclosure Review Process Settlement*, January 5, 2013, available at http://democrats.oversight house.gov/press-releases/house-oversight-committee-requests-briefing-on-potential-independent-foreclosure-review-process-settlement-/ and *Top Democrats Demand Answers on Independent Foreclosure Review Process*, November 18, 2013, available at http://democrats financialservices house.gov/press/PRArticle.aspx?NewsID=1613.

information on the National Mortgage Settlement, see CRS Report R42919, *Oversight and Legal Enforcement of the National Mortgage Settlement*, by David H. Carpenter.

Eminent Domain Proposals

More than five years after the bursting of the housing bubble, cities across the country continue to contend with significant numbers of underwater mortgages that fuel foreclosures and hamper economic recovery. To combat these problems, several city councils across the country, including those of Richmond, CA and North Las Vegas, NV, have entered discussions with a private company, Mortgage Resolution Partners (MRP), to implement eminent domain programs.[52] Although no U.S. city has actually exercised its condemnation powers to effectuate such a plan, the proposals would entail the cities exercising their eminent domain powers to purchase underwater mortgages, selling them to MRP, which would issue new mortgages to the same homeowners for more than their condemnation prices but less than the outstanding principals on the original mortgages. The proposals reportedly would focus on purchasing performing mortgages that are held by private-label (i.e., issued by private companies, not by Fannie Mae, Freddie Mac, or Ginnie Mae), residential mortgage-backed securitized trusts (RMBS trusts). The cities and MRP reportedly would also target homeowners whose newly issued mortgages could qualify for Federal Housing Administration (FHA) insurance.[53]

The Takings Clause of the Fifth Amendment of the U.S. Constitution, which is applicable to states and localities through the Due Process Clause of the Fourteenth Amendment, limits the government's sovereign power to seize private property by eminent domain.[54] States and municipalities also must adhere to their respective state constitutions, almost all of which have analogous provisions.[55] The constitutionally valid exercise of eminent domain requires that two basic principles be met: the private property must be acquired for a "public use"; and the property owner must be paid "just compensation."[56] Although legal challenges against these plans would be very fact specific, the condemnation of underwater mortgages to bolster economic development arguably could raise constitutional questions under both the public use and just compensation principles of state and federal takings clauses.[57]

---

[52] Information on Mortgage Resolution Partners and their "Community Action to Restore Equity and Stability (CARES™)" program is available at http://mortgageresolution.com/. See also Robert Hockett, *Breaking the Mortgage Debt Impasse: Municipal Condemnation Proceedings and Public/Private Partnerships for Mortgage Loan Modification, Value Preservation, and Local Economic Recovery*, Memorandum of Law and Finance, April 21, 2012, available at http://www.lawschool.cornell.edu/spotlights/upload/Memorandum-of-Law-and-Finance-21-April-Municipal-Plan.pdf.

[53] Lydia DePillis, *Richmond's rules: Why one California town is keeping Wall Street up at night*, Washington Post, October 5, 2013, available at http://www.washingtonpost.com/blogs/wonkblog/wp/2013/10/05/richmonds-rules-why-one-california-town-is-keeping-wall-street-up-at-night/.

[54] For a more general discussion of the Takings Clause, see CRS Report RS20741, *The Constitutional Law of Property Rights "Takings": An Introduction*, by Robert Meltz and CRS Report 97-122, *Takings Decisions of the U.S. Supreme Court: A Chronology*, by Robert Meltz.

[55] CRS Report RS20741, *The Constitutional Law of Property Rights "Takings": An Introduction*, by Robert Meltz.

[56] *Id.*

[57] For an analysis of the general constitutional issues raised by these proposals, see CRS Legal Sidebar WSLG620, Constitutional Challenges of Cities' Plans to Acquire Underwater Mortgage by Eminent Domain, by David H. Carpenter. Until a city formally begins implementing an eminent domain program, plaintiffs' constitutional claims against a particular program may not yet be ripe for judicial review. See, for example, Bank of New York Mellon v. City of Richmond, *Order Granting Defendants' Motion to Dismiss*, N.D.Cal., No. 3:13-cv-03664, available at (continued...)

In addition to potential questions regarding their constitutionality, some Members of Congress and other policy makers have expressed policy concerns about plans to acquire underwater mortgages through eminent domain. Critics argue that these proposals would be unfair to mortgage holders, would undermine private contracts, and could be detrimental to future mortgage lending because lenders may be hesitant to offer mortgages in areas that had used eminent domain in the past or may charge higher interest rates to compensate for the perceived increase in risk.[58] Policy makers have called on government agencies, such as FHA, to explain what kind of policies they might adopt if a local jurisdiction proceeded with such a program.[59] Furthermore, legislation has been introduced to prohibit Fannie Mae, Freddie Mac, FHA, and the U.S. Department of Agriculture from backing mortgages on properties located in any area that had used eminent domain to acquire mortgages in the previous 10 years.[60]

For more information on the constitutional issues that may be raised by eminent domain, see CRS Legal Sidebar WSLG187, Legal Questions Abound Proposals to Use Eminent Domain to Acquire Underwater Mortgages, by David H. Carpenter and CRS Legal Sidebar WSLG620, Constitutional Challenges of Cities' Plans to Acquire Underwater Mortgage by Eminent Domain, by David H. Carpenter.

Mortgage Interest Deduction

Moving forward, Congress may continue addressing concerns about the size and sustainability of the recent budget deficits and the country's long-term budget outlook. One place Congress may choose to turn to address these issues is the set of tax benefits for homeowners. Proponents of modifying homeownership tax benefits assert that reducing, modifying, or eliminating all or some of the current tax benefits for homeowners could raise a substantial amount of revenue while simultaneously simplifying the tax code, increasing equity among taxpayers, and promoting economic efficiency.

(...continued)

http://docs.justia.com/cases/federal/district-courts/california/candce/3:2013cv03664/268899/53. The plaintiffs in *Bank of New York Mellon* appealed the district court decision only to withdraw the appeal in May 2014, while reportedly indicating that they would "immediately re-file" the lawsuit if the city moves forward with the implementation of an eminent domain program. See Sam Forgione, *Investors withdraw appeals against California eminent domain plan,* Reuters, May 16, 2014, available at http://www reuters.com/article/2014/05/17/us-mortgages-investing-eminentdomain-idUSBREA4G00A20140517.

[58] See, for example, FHFA General Counsel Memorandum, *Summary of Comments and Additional Analysis Regarding Input on Use of Eminent Domain to Restructure Mortgages,* August 7, 2013, available at http://mba-pac.informz net/mba-pac/data/images/fhfa_gcmemorandumeminentdomain.pdf.

[59] For example, the topic has been raised at congressional hearings and in letters from Members of Congress to federal agencies, including letters to the Secretary of HUD dated June 11, 2013 and November 27, 2013. Both letters are available on the Mortgage Bankers Association's website at http://www mbaa.org/Advocacy/EminentDomainResourceCenter htm. Additionally, the committee reports accompanying the FY2014 Transportation-Housing and Urban Development appropriations bills include language related to eminent domain. The House committee report (H.Rept. 113-136) expresses concern over the proposals and would instruct HUD to submit a study on the effects that it could have on housing and mortgage markets. The Senate committee report (S.Rept. 113-45) indicates that the committee will "continue to monitor developments" related to the use of eminent domain and expects FHA to keep the committee informed of any policies it would pursue if a city moved forward with an eminent domain proposal.

[60] See, for example, H.R. 4745 §233, H.R. 2733, and H.R. 2767 §§108 and 266.

While it is unclear at this point if Congress will make any housing policy tax changes, recent and past proposals have focused on the mortgage interest deduction. Numerous proposals have been offered, from eliminating the deduction altogether, to limiting the deduction to primary residences (i.e., disallowing the deduction for eligible second homes), to converting the deduction to a tax credit, among others. Some are concerned, however, that the economy and housing market are still too weak to start scaling back homeowner tax benefits. Others have suggested that a gradual reduction over time of the available tax benefits would give the market time to adjust and reduce uncertainty among current and potential homeowners.

For example, in 2013, members of the House Committee on Ways and Means were assigned to one of 11 bipartisan groups that were to focus on reforming particular parts of the tax code. One of those groups was tasked with examining reform options for the tax treatment of real estate, including the mortgage interest deduction. Comments solicited from interested parties varied and included support of retaining the deduction as is, permanently expanding the deduction to include private mortgage insurance, converting the deduction to a credit, and reducing the size of mortgage eligible for the deduction, among others.[61]

For more detail on the various proposals that have been made, along with estimated budget effects, see CRS Report R41918, *The Mortgage Interest and Property Tax Deductions: Brief Overview with Revenue Estimates*, by Mark P. Keightley. For an analysis of the rationales for subsidizing homeownership, and an analysis of the effect of current tax incentives on the homeownership rate, see CRS Report R41596, *The Mortgage Interest and Property Tax Deductions: Analysis and Options*, by Mark P. Keightley.

Tax Deduction for Mortgage Insurance Premiums

Traditionally, homeowners have been able to deduct the interest paid on their mortgage, as well as any property taxes they pay as long as they itemize their tax deductions. Beginning in 2007, homeowners could also deduct qualifying mortgage insurance premiums as a result of the Tax Relief and Health Care Act of 2006 (P.L. 109-432). Specifically, homeowners could effectively treat qualifying mortgage insurance premiums as mortgage interest, thus making the premiums deductible if the homeowner itemized, and if the homeowner's adjusted gross income was below a certain threshold ($55,000 for single, and $110,000 for married filing jointly). Originally, the deduction was to only be available for 2007, but it was extended through 2010 by the Mortgage Forgiveness Debt Relief Act of 2007 (P.L. 110-142). The deduction was extended again through 2011 by the Tax Relief, Unemployment Insurance Reauthorization, and Job Creation Act (P.L. 111-312) and most recently through the end of 2013 by the American Taxpayer Relief Act of 2012 (P.L. 112-240).

On April 3, 2014, the Senate Finance Committee passed the Expiring Provisions Improvement Reform and Efficiency Act (EXPIRE; S. 2260), which would extend the deduction for mortgage insurance premiums through 2015.

---

[61] U.S. Congress, Joint Committee on Taxation, *Report to the House Committee on Ways and Means on Present Law and Suggestions for Reform Submitted to the Tax Reform Working Groups*, committee print, 113th Cong., 1st sess., May 6, 2013, JCS-3-13 (Washington: GPO, 2013), p. 541.

Tax Exclusion for Canceled Mortgage Debt Income

A home foreclosure, mortgage default, or mortgage modification can have important tax consequences. As lenders and borrowers work to resolve indebtedness issues, some transactions are resulting in cancellation of debt. Mortgage debt cancellation can occur when lenders restructure loans, reducing principal balances; or sell properties, either in advance, or as a result, of foreclosure proceedings. Historically, if a lender forgives or cancels such debt, tax law has treated it as cancellation of debt (COD) income subject to tax. Exceptions have been available for taxpayers who are insolvent or in bankruptcy, among others—these taxpayers may exclude canceled mortgage debt income under existing law.

The Mortgage Forgiveness Debt Relief Act of 2007 (P.L. 110-142) signed into law on December 20, 2007, temporarily excluded qualified COD income. Thus, the act allowed taxpayers who did not qualify for the existing exceptions to exclude COD income. The provision was effective for debt discharged before January 1, 2010. The Emergency Economic Stabilization Act of 2008 (P.L. 110-343) extended the exclusion of COD income to debt discharged before January 1, 2013. Most recently, the American Taxpayer Relief Act of 2012 (P.L. 112-240) extended the exclusion through the end of 2013.

On April 3, 2014, the Senate Finance Committee passed the Expiring Provisions Improvement Reform and Efficiency Act (EXPIRE; S. 2260), which would extend the exclusion through 2015.

Issues Related to Housing for Low-Income Individuals and Families

The 113th Congress has also been deliberating a number of issues related to housing assistance programs and policies. In general, housing assistance programs are targeted to lower-income households or special populations who have difficulty finding affordable housing. Several issues being considered by Congress are related to funding for housing assistance programs and possible reforms to certain programs.

Appropriations for Housing Assistance Programs

Concern in Congress about reducing federal budget deficits has led to increased interest in reducing the amount of discretionary funding provided each year through the annual appropriations process. Reflecting this interest, the Budget Control Act of 2011 (P.L. 112-25), as amended, implemented discretionary spending caps for FY2012-FY2021, which are designed to reduce growth in discretionary spending. The desire to limit discretionary spending has implications for the Department of Housing and Urban Development's (HUD's) budget, since it is made up almost entirely of discretionary appropriations.

More than three-quarters of HUD's appropriations are devoted to three programs: Section 8 Housing Choice Voucher program rental assistance vouchers, Section 8 project-based rental assistance subsidies, and the public housing program. Funding for Section 8 vouchers makes up the largest share of HUD's budget, accounting for nearly half. The cost of the Section 8 voucher program has been growing in recent years since Congress has created more vouchers each year over the past several years (largely to replace units lost to the affordable housing stock in other assisted housing programs), and since the cost of renewing individual vouchers has been growing as gaps between low-income tenants' incomes and rents in the market have been growing.[62] The cost of the project-based Section 8 program has also been growing in recent years as more and more long-term rental assistance contracts on older properties expire and are renewed, requiring new appropriations.[63] Public housing, the third-largest expense in HUD's budget, has, arguably, been underfunded (based on studies undertaken by HUD of what it should cost to operate and maintain public housing)[64] for many years, which means there is regular pressure from low-income housing advocates and others to increase funding for public housing.

In a budget environment featuring limits on discretionary spending, the pressure to provide more funding for HUD's largest programs must be balanced against the pressure from states, localities, and advocates to maintain or increase funding for other HUD programs, such as the Community Development Block Grant (CDBG) program, grants for homelessness assistance, and funding for Native American housing.

Further, HUD's funding needs must be considered in the context of those for the Department of Transportation. Funding levels for HUD, along with those of the Department of Transportation (DOT), are determined by the Transportation, HUD, and Related Agencies (T-HUD) appropriations subcommittee, generally in a bill by the same name. While the DOT's overall budget is generally larger than HUD's, because the majority of DOT's budget is made up of mandatory funding, HUD's budget makes up the largest share of the discretionary T-HUD appropriations bill each year.

For more information about HUD appropriations, see the CRS Issue Before Congress website, "Transportation, HUD, and Related Agencies' Appropriations."[65] For more information about the Budget Control Act, see CRS Report R41965, *The Budget Control Act of 2011*, by Bill Heniff Jr., Elizabeth Rybicki, and Shannon M. Mahan, and for more information about trends in funding for HUD, see CRS Report R42542, *Department of Housing and Urban Development (HUD): Funding Trends Since FY2002*, by Maggie McCarty.

Assisted Housing Reform

Over most of the past decade, Congress has considered reforms to the nation's two largest direct housing assistance programs: the Section 8 Housing Choice Voucher and public housing programs. The majority of these reforms are aimed at streamlining the programs' administration, although some have been farther reaching than others. Recent reform proposals, including those

---

[62] For more information about how these factors are driving cost growth in the Section 8 Housing Choice Voucher program, see U.S. Government Accountability Office (GAO), *Housing Choice Vouchers: Options Exist to Increase Program Efficiencies*, GAO-12-2003, March 19, 2012, http://www.gao.gov/products/GAO-12-300.

[63] For more information about the Section 8 project-based rental assistance program, see CRS Report RL32284, *An Overview of the Section 8 Housing Programs: Housing Choice Vouchers and Project-Based Rental Assistance*, by Maggie McCarty.

[64] For example, see Meryl Finkel et. al., "Capital Needs in the Public Housing Program: Revised Final Report," prepared for the Department of Housing and Urban Development, November 24, 2010, http://portal hud.gov/hudportal/documents/huddoc?id=PH_Capital_Needs.pdf.

[65] The "Transportation, HUD, and Related Agencies Appropriations" Issue Before Congress website is at http://crs.gov/pages/subissue.aspx?cliid=2351&parentid=73&preview=False.

considered in the 111th and 112th Congresses, have included a number of fairly uncontroversial administrative provisions, along with others that have proved more controversial.

The Section 8 Housing Choice Voucher program is HUD's largest direct housing assistance program for low-income families, both in terms of the number of families it serves (over 2 million) and the amount of money it costs (over $18 billion in FY2013, about half of HUD's total appropriation). The program is administered at the local level, by public housing authorities (PHAs), and provides vouchers—portable rental subsidies—to very low-income families, which they can use to reduce their rents in the private market units of their choice (subject to certain cost limits). The program has been criticized for, among other issues, its administrative complexity and growing cost.[66]

The public housing program has existed longer than the Section 8 voucher program and is now smaller in size, with over 1 million units of low-rent public housing available to eligible low-income tenants. Public housing is owned by the same local PHAs that administer the Section 8 voucher program and those PHAs receive annual operating and capital funding from Congress through HUD. Much of the public housing stock is old and in need of capital repairs. According to the most recent study conducted by HUD, addressing the outstanding physical needs of the public housing stock would cost nearly $26 billion.[67] The amount Congress typically provides in annual appropriations for capital needs has not been sufficient to address that backlog. In response, PHAs have increasingly relied on other sources of financing, particularly private market loans, to meet the capital needs of their housing stock. However, there are limits on the extent to which PHAs can borrow funds; most notably, they are generally restricted by federal rules from mortgaging their public housing properties. Further, the public housing program has, like the voucher program, been criticized for being overly complex and burdensome to administer, especially in light of recent funding reductions.

Recent reform proposals have included changes to the income eligibility and rent determination process for both programs, designed to make it less complicated, and changes to the physical inspection process in the voucher program to give PHAs more options for reducing the frequency of inspections and increasing sanctions for failed inspections. Proposed legislation has also included changes to the formula by which voucher funding is allocated to PHAs. In recent years, annual appropriations laws have specified different formulas for allocating voucher funding; voucher reform legislation has sought to codify a permanent formula (although, even if enacted it could still be overridden in the appropriations acts). Finally, recent reform proposals have included modifications to and expansions of the Moving to Work (MTW) demonstration, which permits a selected group of PHAs to seek waivers of most federal rules and regulations governing the Section 8 voucher program and the public housing program.

No reform legislation has been introduced in the 113th Congress. However, the President has requested in his past several budget submissions that Congress enact several of the less controversial administrative reforms (for example, those related to income calculation and

---

[66] U.S. Government Accountability Office (GAO), *Housing Choice Vouchers: Options Exist to Increase Program Efficiencies*, GAO-12-2003, March 19, 2012, http://www.gao.gov/products/GAO-12-300.

[67] Meryl Finkel et. al., "Capital Needs in the Public Housing Program: Revised Final Report," prepared for the Department of Housing and Urban Development, November 24, 2010, http://portal.hud.gov/hudportal/documents/huddoc?id=PH_Capital_Needs.pdf.

verification) as a part of the annual appropriations acts. The FY2014 Omnibus funding measure (P.L. 113-76) included several administrative reforms.[68]

For more information, see CRS Report RL34002, *Section 8 Housing Choice Voucher Program: Issues and Reform Proposals*, by Maggie McCarty.

Reauthorization of the Native American Housing Assistance and Self-Determination Act (NAHASDA)

The Native American Housing Assistance and Self-Determination Act of 1996 (NAHASDA) reorganized the system of federal housing assistance for Native Americans living in tribal areas. NAHASDA terminated the ability of tribes to receive assistance under several existing HUD programs, and consolidated most housing funding for tribes into a single block grant program, the Native American Housing Block Grant (NAHBG).[69] Federally recognized tribes and Alaska Native villages are eligible to receive formula funding under the NAHBG to use for a variety of housing activities that benefit low-income households living in the tribe's formula area.

In addition to the block grant program, NAHASDA also authorized a loan guarantee program under which HUD provides a guarantee on certain eligible loans made to tribes for housing-related purposes (the Title VI Loan Guarantee Program), as well as funding for training and technical assistance. A block grant program similar to the NAHBG, the Native Hawaiian Housing Block Grant (NHHBG), provides funds for affordable housing for low-income Native Hawaiians who are eligible to live on the Hawaiian home lands and is also authorized under NAHASDA, as amended.

NAHASDA's authorization expired at the end of FY2013. A bill to reauthorize NAHASDA programs has been introduced in the Senate (S. 1352) and was reported out of the Senate Committee on Indian Affairs in January 2014. Two NAHASDA reauthorization bills (H.R. 4277 and H.R. 4329) have been introduced in the House and have been referred to the House Financial Services Committee. The three bills are different from one another, although some similar provisions are included in all three. For example, all three bills would authorize programs to provide housing vouchers to Native American veterans residing on or near Native American lands who are homeless or at risk of homelessness. Two of the bills, S. 1352 and H.R. 4277, would reauthorize the Native Hawaiian Housing Block Grant along with the NAHBG; H.R. 4329 would not reauthorize the Native Hawaiian program.[70]

---

[68] Including the establishment of flat rents for public housing (Division L, Title II, Section 210), the redefinition of "public housing authority" to include consortia (Division L, Title II, Section 212), the modification of Section 8 voucher inspection requirements (Division L, Title II, Section 220), the redefinition of "extremely low-income" (Division L, Title II, Section 238), and the modification of utility allowances for Section 8 voucher holders (Division L, Title II, Section 242).

[69] The NAHBG is sometimes also referred to as the Indian Housing Block Grant, or IHBG.

[70] The Native Hawaiian Housing Block Grant has not been reauthorized since FY2005, although it has continued to receive funding in annual appropriations acts. Some policy makers have opposed reauthorizing the NHHBG on the grounds that, unlike federally recognized Indian tribes, Native Hawaiians are not a sovereign political entity. Therefore, some have argued that the NHHBG could be perceived to be providing funds on the basis of race, a constitutionally suspect basis, rather than political status as members of sovereign tribes.

For more information on NAHASDA, see CRS Report R43307, *The Native American Housing Assistance and Self-Determination Act of 1996 (NAHASDA): Background and Funding*, by Katie Jones.

Definition of "Rural" in Rural Housing Programs

The U.S. Department of Agriculture (USDA) administers a number of housing assistance programs for low and moderate income residents of rural areas. They include rental housing development and rent subsidy programs, as well as single-family direct loan and mortgage insurance programs. These programs are only available in "rural" areas, as defined by the authorizing statute for the programs.[71] That definition is complicated, and involves maximum population thresholds, and in some cases a determination by USDA that the area is "rural in character" and lacks access to mortgage credit. Further, in past years, Congress has modified the definition to allow certain areas to continue to be considered rural, despite exceeding population thresholds based on updated decennial Census data.[72]

With the release of Census 2010 population figures, the USDA updated the list of areas to be designated as rural, reflecting the new Census data. According to preliminary estimates released by USDA in 2012, over 900 communities that were identified as "rural" would have no longer met the criteria and would thus have lost eligibility to participate in rural housing programs.[73]

USDA was initially planning to begin using the updated list of eligible communities at the start of FY2013. However, Congress included in the FY2013 appropriations law language maintaining eligibility for rural housing programs in any communities that were considered eligible for participation at the end of FY2012.[74] This "grandfathering" of existing eligible communities was extended through the end of FY2014 under the terms of the final FY2014 Omnibus appropriations law (P.L. 113-76).[75]

Following enactment of P.L. 113-76, the Agricultural Act of 2014, also known as the 2014 "Farm Bill" (P.L. 113-79), amended the statutory definition of rural. The amendment (1) extends the existing provisions disregarding 1990 and 2000 decennial Census data in determining certain communities' rural status to also disregard 2010 decennial Census data; and (2) expands the

---

[71] 42 U.S.C. §1490.

[72] Specifically, the definition, prior to enactment of the 2014 Farm Bill, included the following clause: "For purposes of this title, any area classified as 'rural' or a 'rural area' prior to October 1, 1990, and determined not to be 'rural' or a 'rural area' as a result of data received from or after the 1990 or 2000 decennial census shall continue to be so classified until the receipt of data from the decennial census in the year 2010, if such area has a population in excess of 10,000 but not in excess of 25,000, is rural in character, and has a serious lack of mortgage credit for lower and moderate-income families." (42 U.S.C. §1490)

[73] USDA's preliminary list of communities that would lose eligibility for rural housing programs is available on the National Rural Housing Coalition's website at http://ruralhousingcoalition.org/wp-content/uploads/2012/02/USDA-List-of-Impacted-Communities_06272012.pdf.

[74] See Section 731 of P.L. 113-6.

[75] See Section 737, Division A, Title VII, which states: "None of the funds made available by this Act may be used to reclassify any area eligible for rural housing programs of the Rural Housing Service on September 30, 2013 as not eligible for such programs."

population threshold for the purposes of retaining eligibility for certain communities from 25,000 to 35,000.[76]

For more information about USDA rural housing programs, see CRS Report RL31837, *An Overview of USDA Rural Development Programs*, by Tadlock Cowan.

Low-Income Housing Tax Credit

The low-income housing tax credit (LIHTC) program is one of the federal government's primary policy tools for encouraging the development and rehabilitation of affordable rental housing. These non-refundable federal housing tax credits are awarded to developers of qualified rental projects via a competitive application process administered by state housing finance agencies. Developers typically sell their tax credits to outside investors in exchange for equity. Selling the tax credits reduces the debt developers would otherwise have to incur and the equity they would otherwise have to contribute. With lower financing costs, tax credit properties can potentially offer lower, more affordable rents.

The Housing and Economic Recovery Act of 2008 (P.L. 110-289) temporarily changed the formula used to determine how many LIHTCs new rental construction is awarded. The act increased the potential number of credits a LIHTC property could receive by ensuring that new construction receives LIHTCs of no less than 9% multiplied by a property's eligible basis (eligible costs). Most recently, the American Taxpayer Relief Act of 2012 (P.L. 112-240) extended the 9% floor for credit allocations made before January 1, 2014. On April 3, 2014, the Senate Finance Committee passed the Expiring Provisions Improvement Reform and Efficiency Act (EXPIRE; S. 2260), which would extend the 9% floor and establish a temporary 4% floor for rehabilitated housing. Both provisions would expire at the end of 2015.

The LIHTC program could experience changes if tax reform were to take place in the 113th Congress. In 2013, members of the House Committee on Ways and Means were assigned to one of 11 bipartisan groups that were to focus on reforming particular parts of the tax code. One of those groups was tasked with examining reform options for the tax treatment of real estate, including the LIHTC program. Comments solicited from interested parties appear to support retaining the program, and in some cases enhancing the credit's value.[77] At the same time, some have raised questions as to the program's cost effectiveness and its ability to increase the net supply of affordable housing.

Housing Trust Fund

For many years, affordable housing advocates, led by the National Low-Income Housing Coalition (NLIHC), had argued for the creation of a national housing trust fund to provide a dedicated source of funding outside of the annual appropriations process that could be used for the production of rental housing for the lowest-income households. In 2008, Congress established the Housing Trust Fund in the Housing and Economic Recovery Act of 2008 (P.L. 110-289).

---

[76] See 42 U.S.C. §1490 or footnote 72 for the current definition. The provision can be found in Section 6208 of the law.

[77] U.S. Congress, Joint Committee on Taxation, *Report to the House Committee on Ways and Means on Present Law and Suggestions for Reform Submitted to the Tax Reform Working Groups*, committee print, 113th Cong., 1st sess., May 6, 2013, JCS-3-13 (Washington: GPO, 2013), p. 538.

Through the Housing Trust Fund, HUD would provide formula-based grants to states to use primarily for rental housing for very low- and extremely low-income households.[78] The dedicated funding source for the Housing Trust Fund was to be contributions from Fannie Mae and Freddie Mac. However, before the Housing Trust Fund had ever received any funding, the contributions were suspended by the Federal Housing Finance Agency (FHFA) after Fannie Mae and Freddie Mac were placed into conservatorship.

The Housing Trust Fund has not been funded to date. Affordable housing advocates have continued to seek a source of funding for the Housing Trust Fund and have suggested a number of possible funding sources.[79] Most recently, as Fannie Mae and Freddie Mac have once again become profitable,[80] advocates have argued that their contributions to the Housing Trust Fund should be reinstated and have initiated legal action to attempt to require Fannie Mae and Freddie Mac to begin making contributions.[81] Some policy makers, however, have opposed the Housing Trust Fund since its creation, arguing that it is duplicative of other housing programs or that its funds could be misused.[82] There have been legislative proposals in the current and recent Congresses to eliminate the Housing Trust Fund entirely. For example, the PATH Act, discussed earlier in this report, would repeal the Housing Trust Fund.[83]

For more information on the Housing Trust Fund, see CRS Report R40781, *The Housing Trust Fund: Background and Issues*, by Katie Jones.

---

[78] Very low-income households are defined as households with incomes at or below 50% of area median income (AMI), and extremely low-income families are defined as households with incomes at or below 30% of AMI.

[79] For a list of proposed funding sources from the National Low-Income Housing Coalition, see http://nlihc.org/sites/default/files/NHTF_Funding.pdf.

[80] See CRS Report R42760, *Fannie Mae's and Freddie Mac's Financial Status: Frequently Asked Questions*, by N. Eric Weiss.

[81] See the National Low-Income Housing Coalition's website at http://nlihc.org/issues/nhtf/lawsuit.

[82] For example, see Representative Ed Royce's July 12, 2011, press release describing his bill to eliminate the Housing Trust Fund during the 112th Congress at http://royce house.gov/news/documentsingle.aspx?DocumentID=251288.

[83] H.R. 2767 §104.

Author Contact Information

Katie Jones, Coordinator
Analyst in Housing Policy
kmjones@crs.loc.gov, 7-4162

David H. Carpenter
Legislative Attorney
dcarpenter@crs.loc.gov, 7-9118

Sean M. Hoskins
Analyst in Financial Economics
shoskins@crs.loc.gov, 7-8958

Mark P. Keightley
Specialist in Economics
mkeightley@crs.loc.gov, 7-1049

Maggie McCarty
Specialist in Housing Policy
mmccarty@crs.loc.gov, 7-2163

N. Eric Weiss
Specialist in Financial Economics
eweiss@crs.loc.gov, 7-6209

Key Policy Staff

Area of Expertise	Name	Phone	E-mail
Community and economic development, including Community Development Block Grants, Brownfields, empowerment zones	Eugene Boyd	7-8689	eboyd@crs.loc.gov
Consumer law, banking law, foreclosure law, and mortgage lending	David H. Carpenter	7-9118	dcarpenter@crs.loc.gov
Housing law, including fair housing	Jody Feder	7-8088	jfeder@crs.loc.gov
	Jane Smith	7-7202	jmsmith@crs.loc.gov
General mortgage finance issues, including credit availability and underwriting	Darryl E. Getter	7-2834	dgetter@crs.loc.gov
Housing finance issues, including mortgage servicing	Sean M. Hoskins	7-8958	shoskins@crs.loc.gov
Foreclosure mitigation, FHA, Housing Trust Fund, HOME, Native American housing programs	Katie Jones	7-4162	kmjones@crs.loc.gov
Housing tax policy, including the Low-Income Housing Tax Credit, mortgage revenue bonds, and other tax incentives for rental housing and owner-occupied housing	Mark Patrick Keightley	7-1049	mkeightley@crs.loc.gov
Emergency management policy, including post-disaster FEMA temporary housing issues and FEMA's Emergency Food and Shelter Program	Francis X. McCarthy	7-9533	fmccarthy@crs.loc.gov
Assisted rental housing, including Section 8, public and assisted housing, assisted housing preservation, rural housing, and HUD appropriations	Maggie McCarty	7-2163	mmccarty@crs.loc.gov
Banking and securities regulation, including mortgage finance	Edward Vincent Murphy	7-6201	tmurphy@crs.loc.gov

Area of Expertise	Name	Phone	E-mail
Housing for special populations, including persons who are elderly, disabled, homeless, HOPWA, veterans' housing	Libby Perl	7-7806	eperl@crs.loc.gov
Fannie Mae, Freddie Mac, Federal Home Loan Banks, and housing finance	N. Eric Weiss	7-6209	eweiss@crs.loc.gov

www.ingramcontent.com/pod-product-compliance
Lightning Source LLC
Chambersburg PA
CBHW081137280526
45787CB00007B/3113

9781505552928